Saving Susie

An Elder Abuse Horror Story

By Nancy Richmond

ISBN-13: 978-1500187569

ISBN-10: 1500187569

CONTENTS

Forward

According to the World Health Organization, elder abuse is defined as "a single, or repeated act, or lack of appropriate action, occurring within any relationship where there is an expectation of trust which causes harm or distress to an older person."

They further state "Elder Abuse can take various forms such as physical, sexual psychological, emotional, or financial abuse. It can also be the result of intentional or unintentional neglect. Until recently, this serious social problem was hidden from the public view and considered mostly a private matter. Even today, elder abuse continues to be a taboo, mostly underestimated and ignored by societies across the world. Evidence is accumulating, however, to indicate that elder abuse is an important public health and societal problem."

The perpetrators of elder abuse are usually family members, care givers or close acquaintances. My own mother suffered terrible elder abuse from family members for nearly a year. This is her story. In order to prevent claims of libel, I have provided documentation of every incidence of abuse that my mother suffered in an appendix at the back of this book, since the judicial system of

this country considers truth to be the

ultimate defense against libel. If a statement

can be proven to be true, then there is no

libel.

It is my hope that this book may help

in some small way to promote awareness of,

and perhaps some day, to end elder abuse.

Nancy Richmond

This book is dedicated with love to my

mother Susie George and to Patsy, her

"Angel Unaware."

CHAPTER ONE

Quinwood, West Virginia is a charming little community nestled deep within the heart of the Appalachian Mountain Range. It came into existence as a coal camp in the early nineteen hundreds, and was incorporated as a town in 1947. When the coal industry declined, the local population grew smaller, but its remaining citizens stayed true to their early roots and southern culture.

Quinwood today still boasts several businesses as well as an elementary school, a library, an ambulance service and a volunteer fire department. There is a homeless shelter, Hope Haven, and a food pantry. Everyone in the little town knows everyone else, and most are eager to lend a helping hand in times of trouble. With a population that fluctuates between 200 and 400, it is the kind of place that many people who live there consider to be 'almost heaven'.

Susie and Aldon George and their six children, Patsy, David, Mary, Nancy, Connie and Janice Rebecca (known as Becky) moved into the vicinity of Quinwood in the early 1950s. Aldon's grandfather, George Washington George, was the first resident of the coal camp when it was formed, so they were familiar with the area.

In the 1970s, Susie and Aldon bought several acres of land near the center of Quinwood, and put a double wide trailer on it, making it their retirement home. The property included a ramshackle old house when they purchased it, which Aldon later remodeled as a guest house.

At one time their daughter Nancy and her two little girls lived there, and a few years later, when their youngest daughter Becky married Bobby Jones, they gave the house to the couple as a wedding gift.

Susie George was a small woman who stood just over five feet tall and weighed around 100 pounds. Her olive complection, jet black hair and dark brown eyes made her stand out in any crowd, and she was high spirited and always ready for an adventure.

Susie was a second generation Scotts Irish American. Her grandfather James Burdiss came to America from Scotland aboard the Passenger Ship 'The West Point' and landed in New York Harbor in 1848. Susie was born in 1923, just before the time of the Great Depression, to a coal mining family who lived near Beckley, WV.

One of twelve children, Susie's life was never easy. She had only a fourth grade education because from the time she was 10, she had to stay home and help her mom with the household chores. She spent her childhood years in a shanty beside the railroad tracks; cooking, cleaning and washing the dirty, dusty clothes that her father and older brothers who worked in the mines brought home every night.

Susie also helped care for the younger members of the family. She had a beautiful voice and spent hours singing to her little brothers and sisters. She loved children and enjoyed taking care of them.

By the time she was sixteen, Susie had met and was being courted by Aldon George, a young man from a farm near Quinwood. They became engaged, but the advent of World War Two separated the couple when Aldon joined the army and was stationed in Omar, Africa for two years.

Susie was nineteen when Aldon returned home. They were married by a justice of the peace in Rainelle, WV and rented a small house there. Aldon obtained employment as a coal miner, and he and

Susie moved from town to town in Greenbrier County for several years, following the trail of mines that constantly opened and closed in the area.

Susie desperately wanted to start a family, but when she had not conceived by the time she was twenty-five, the doctors told her that she would probably never have children. So she was delighted when she found out that she was expecting in 1947.

Tragically, there were complications during the birth and the doctor had to use forceps in the delivery. The baby, whom they named Patsy Sue, suffered a concussion from the instrument, and her brain began to swell, causing irreversible brain damage.

The prognosis for the baby's survival was poor, but eventually the swelling went down and Patsy began to thrive. Susie was heart broken that her baby was so badly injured. She spent all her waking hours seeing that the tiny girl was loved and nurtured. She devoted herself to Patsy, to insure that her daughter had the best life it was possible for her to live. Patsy would never progress mentally much further than a three year old child, but she had a sweet and sunny nature and was a joy to be around.

Her favorite things were coloring and playing Old Maid cards with her family.

As she grew older, Patsy began to have trouble keeping her balance, and could not walk without assistance, so she spent most of her time sitting in her oversized chair watching television. She was a gentle and docile girl who never caused any trouble for her parents and was always anxious to please whomever she was with.

Susie and Aldon went on to have five more children. By 1952 they had bought a house in Marfrance, about two miles from Quinwood, where they lived and raised their family. Susie had her hands full, especially with the problems that having a special needs child involved.

Susie never learned to drive, and depended on Aldon to take her to the store once a week. Her husband also managed all the family finances, which was common in that generation, so Susie did not know how to balance a check book or pay bills.

Susie was fiercely protective of Patsy, and she often told her other children when they tried to exclude her "If Patsy doesn't play, then nobody plays." For Susie, Patsy would always be a little two year old girl with dark curly hair and an angelic laugh.

From the time she was young, Susie was a devout Christian. She never swore or drank, and was honest and truthful in everything she did. She tried to instill those values into her children as they grew. She often read them stories from the Bible, quoting her favorite verses to them whenever it seemed appropriate. If they misbehaved, Susie would reprimand them, saying " Even if no one else sees you being bad, God does. Nothing you do is hidden forever. The Bible says *'Be sure your sins will find you out'* and they always do."

In 1968 Susie became ill and was diagnosed with uterine cancer. The doctors did not think she would survive, so they asked her to participate in a medical trial of experimental new chemotherapy drugs, which might be able to save her. She agreed and took the drugs, which caused her hair to fall out and her skin to blister. She was hospitalized for over a month, and lost 20 pounds, but her will to live was so strong that eventually she overcame the cancer and was pronounced cured, and was able to return home and resume her life.

By the time the family moved into

their new double wide trailer in Quinwood,

the three oldest children had already left

home. Aldon, now retired, grew a garden in

the backyard every summer, while Susie

spent her time caring for the three girls who

were still at home, attending church, and

occasionally going to Bingo at the VFW

building in the nearby town of Rainelle.

In time, Susie's daughters Connie

and Becky married. Becky and her husband

Bobby moved into the small house next to

Susie and Aldon's trailer. Whenever Aldon

was busy or ill, Becky would drive her

mother to town or to the beauticians, where

Susie had her hair done every week.

In the early months of 1982, Susie's beloved husband Aldon died of a massive heart attack. Not only had Susie lost the love of her life and her companion of almost 40 years, at the age of 59 she no longer had the only person who was responsible for keeping the family finances in order, and for driving her and Patsy everywhere they went.

Since Becky lived next door, she was the logical person to take over those duties, and Susie trusted her completely. Becky's husband Bobby did handy man jobs and kept the lawn mowed at the trailer, and

Susie made sure that they were both well compensated for the help they gave her.

Susie still did all her own housework and cared for Patsy, just as she had always done. The arrangement seemed to work well, and whenever Becky was not available, Nancy or Connie would drive their mother wherever she needed to go. Susie's two older children, David and Mary, lived in Ohio. They would both come in once or twice a year to visit, and often took Susie and Patsy on vacation to the beach.

Eventually, Susie became a grandmother and doted on her grandchildren.

Patsy loved them all, and would hold them and feed them (with Susie's help) when they visited. As they got older, the grandchildren enjoyed spending time with Patsy and considered her their playmate. When they became teenagers, Nancy's daughters Tammy and Misty would often stay with Patsy when Susie went to church or Bingo.

For nearly fifteen years after Aldon's death, Susie and Patsy continued to live in their modest home in Quinwood. Because of the time she spent caring for her disabled daughter, Susie had very few friends, relying on her family for companionship. She was very frugal and over the years managed to

save a large sum of money from the Social

Security and UMWA pension checks she and

Patsy both received each month. Being a

child of the Depression era, she did not

entirely trust banks, so although she kept a

checking account and had several bank

CD's, she also secreted a large amount of

cash away in a safe deposit box.

   While Susie still missed her husband

terribly, she was content to live in the home

they had shared for so many years, and

devoted herself to taking care of Patsy,

whom she fondly referred to as her 'angel

unaware.'

But in January of 1997, the year Susie turned 74, she was incapacitated for several months because of a severe allergic reaction. Tragically, her illness set in motion a series of events that would make her a victim of a vicious cycle of elder abuse from those she trusted most.

CHAPTER TWO

During the late 1980s and early

1990s, Quinwood experienced a resurgence

of population and income due to a dramatic

rise in the number of coal mining operations

in Greenbrier County, WV. The mining

companies were recruiting men at a rapid

pace, and paying top wages for experienced

workers.

However, the boom in the coal

market was followed by a severe slump in

the late 1990s, and most of the mines around

Quinwood shut down, laying off hundreds of

men. Many of those families faced financial

ruin, since there were few other jobs available in the area, and none that offered even half of the wages that the mines paid.

Bobby Jones, the husband of Susie's youngest daughter Becky, was one of the men who lost his job, and both he and Becky were unemployed during 1996. Susie was happy to come to the aid of the struggling couple, letting Becky write checks from her account to buy groceries and pay their utility bills.

Shortly after Christmas that year, Susie was diagnosed with lung cancer and liver disease. During a routine CAT scan at the hospital, she was injected with an iodine solution that was used for contrast in the scan. Unfortunately, no one knew that Susie was allergic to iodine, and she had a very bad reaction to it. Susie was confined to her bed, and could not care for herself or for Patsy. She was very weak and at times almost unresponsive. She lost weight and had difficulty keeping any food down. Family members began to fear that she would not recover from the allergic reaction.

Because someone had to be available at all times to care for both Susie and Patsy, her daughters Becky, Connie and Nancy took turns helping out and staying at the trailer at night. Occasionally, one of Susie's adult grand children would come by and run errands or do housework.

Eventually, Becky and Bobby moved into Susie's trailer. It seemed to be an ideal solution, since it would help them financially and also provide someone to look after Susie and Patsy on a full time basis.

Susie's youngest daughter Becky was a small, extremely thin woman with slightly stooped shoulders and eyes that perpetually squinted due to her extreme nearsightedness. Becky was born with a heart defect, and was spoiled by her parents, who feared she might not survive, so she learned at an early age to manipulate her family into giving her whatever she wanted. Becky and her husband Bobby, a middle aged man of average height and build who had a receding hairline and a slight paunch, were considered by the residents of Quinwood to be good Samaritans for taking on the job of looking after Susie and Patsy in their time of need.

However, within just a few weeks of moving into Susie's home, Becky began making plans to transfer all of Susie's assets to herself. She recruited the aid of her

brother David, who lived in Ohio, to carry
out her plans.

David, Susie's only son, had been put
through college by his parents and had
taught school for a year, then attended
seminary to be a pastor. He then left the
church to work with handicapped people.
He had been married and divorced twice, and
had no children. David was a slender,
bookish man with a sixties style 'Beetle' hair
cut and very pale skin. He was quiet and
reserved, and devoted to his sister Becky.

The siblings had a legal document
drawn up by a local lawyer giving David and

Becky a power of attorney over Susie.

David made the six hour journey to West

Virginia, and on the 19th of January, he and

Becky drove Susie to the Quinwood Public

Library, where their mother signed the

document in the presence of the librarian,

who was also a Notary Public.

Armed with the power of attorney,

the pair then attempted to transfer Susie's

property to into their names, but they ran

into an unexpected obstacle.

When Aldon and Susie bought their

land, they had the deed made out to Aldon,

Susie, and Patsy, which meant that David

and Becky would need a power of attorney for Patsy in order to transfer the deed to themselves.

But under state law, Patsy was considered an incapacitated and incompetent person, and could not legally sign a power of attorney. Undeterred, Becky had an unsigned power of attorney drawn up, and on the seventh of February, she arranged for a personal friend, Debra Pomeroy O'Dell (now Debra Callsion) who was a Notary Public, to witness Patsy signing the document.

Debra had known Patsy all her life,

she lived across the street from the George family in Quinwood and attended the First Baptist Church with them, so she was well aware that Patsy was not competent to sign the document; but she witnessed Patsy's childish scrawl on the paper anyway, and placed her notary seal on it, giving the siblings an illegal power of attorney for the handicapped girl.

Becky and David then used the two documents to have a new deed made which listed them as co-owners of Lots 17, 18 and 19 in Quinwood, transferring property that was valued at $40,000 to themselves, while paying only ten dollars for it.

Becky Jones also used her mother's power of attorney to withdraw the sum of $79, 257. 08 from Susie's bank account at First State Bank and Trust in Rainelle, and to close the account.

Next, Becky enrolled Patsy as a client with the Seneca Mental Health / Mental Retardation Council, Inc., using her mother's power of attorney to represent herself as Patsy's guardian. The program provided services for adults with mental disabilities, and in Patsy's case, would send workers to her home on a daily basis to "provide skill training, monitoring and supervision designed to assist an individual with developmental disabilities in achieving increased independence or maintaining current skills in activities of daily living." (http://www.shsinc.org/index.html)

Because Seneca often hired and trained family members to provide care for their clients, they agreed to give both Becky and her husband Bobby jobs working with Patsy. The positions offered a good salary as well as medical benefits.

Neither Susie nor any of her family members had any idea that Susie's assets were being systematically removed from her

possession and transferred to her children

Becky Jones and David George, leaving her

destitute and totally at their mercy.

CHAPTER THREE

Although almost everyone, including
her doctors, thought that there was no hope
of recovery for Susie, by June she began to
show signs of improvement. She started
eating more, and had periods of mental
clarity. Before long, she was able to sit in
her recliner in the living room with Patsy,
watching television and occasionally
responding when spoken to.

The next few weeks brought a rapid
recovery for Susie, especially in her ability to
talk and reason. While her body was still
frail and wasted from her age and various

illnesses, which included lung cancer, liver disease and lupus, Susie's indomitable spirit could not be repressed, and she slowly began resuming her previous routine. Before long she was able to dress and bathe herself, and soon she began doing light housework.

Not realizing how she had been taken advantage of, Susie felt grateful for the care that Becky and Bobby had given to her and to Patsy during her illness, and often thanked them for it. But as time went on she began to chaff under their constant presence, and the fact that they continued to treat her as if she were an invalid. She did not like the way that the couple seemed to be in control of her and Patsy's lives, and wanted things to be the way they were before her illness.

At last Susie broached the subject of having Becky and Bobby move back into their own house. After all, it was only a few hundred yards from her own, and she could contact them by phone if she needed help. That is when she first learned that Becky and Bobby were being paid by Seneca to work with Patsy, and that they had no intention of giving up their jobs or leaving her home. When she continued to insist that the couple move out of the trailer, Becky stopped talking to her.

The following morning, Susie woke up feeling groggy and disoriented. Her speech was slurred and she found it hard to keep her balance. The ' sick spell', as she called it, lasted several hours and then slowly went away, leaving her feeling drained and weak.

Soon Susie began having sick spells whenever she argued with Becky, or anytime she was going to be out in public. She did not know it at the time, but Becky and Bobby were giving her double doses of her medications, which made her appear delusional and out of touch with reality to anyone she came in contact with, and which could possibly have been fatal to her in her weakened condition.

Becky told Susie's family, neighbors, and doctors that her mother was suffering from dementia and could not be trusted around Patsy. She discouraged visitors, saying that they only made Susie agitated and upset, and made it harder for her to be controlled.

Still, there was not enough medication to keep Susie sedated all the time, and whenever she was not drugged, she fought with her daughter and son-in-law, trying to make them move out.

On the first of each month, Becky took Susie to the bank to cash her Social Security check. Large amounts of cash began to disappear from Susie's purse, but when she complained, Becky laughed and told her mother that she was just getting senile and didn't remember spending it. Susie became more and more frustrated, but she felt helpless to do anything about it.

On August 18, the situation had become so volatile that Becky took her mother to the Appalachian Regional Hospital and asked to have her admitted to the psychiatric ward for observation, hoping to have her committed for dementia. Susie was treated by Psychiatrist Ahmed D. Faheem.

Becky told the doctor that her mother was severely depressed and suicidal, and that she was threatening to kill her and her husband Bobby. Becky further stated that her mother was suspicious, distrustful and paranoid of everyone, and that she had a gun. Susie denied all the allegations, saying that she did not remember saying any of the things that Becky was accusing her of, nor did she own a firearm.

Susie was admitted into the psychiatric ward for observation, and was kept in the hospital for several days. She told the doctor that "her daughter and son-in law had come in and were trying to make major changes in the family."

The doctor's diagnosis was that although Susie was extremely depressed and was expressing 'significant hopeless, helpless and despondent feelings', her judgement was intact and that there was no looseness of association on her part. He found no reason to keep her incarcerated, and released her from the hospital.

When Susie returned home, the situation became openly hostile. Becky and Bobby ignored her and tried to keep her from having any interaction with Patsy.

Susie began to suspect that she was being drugged, and would only eat or drink from sealed containers that she opened herself. She prayed constantly that God would deliver her from her misery and somehow give her back her life.

The summer wore on and by November the relationship between the family members was stretched to the breaking point. Even Patsy was becoming stressed, not understanding exactly what was happening, but knowing that everyone seemed angry all the time.

One afternoon, Susie's daughter Nancy stopped by to see her mom. Nancy did not visit as often as she had in the past, because of the tension in her mother's home.

When Susie saw her tall, athletic daughter hurrying up the sidewalk, her long blonde hair blowing in the cold November wind, she grabbed her jacket and purse and hurried outside before Becky could stop her.

Susie asked Nancy to drive her into Rainelle to shop. Nancy was more than willing to do so, and was happy to see that her mother seemed to be doing so well.

During the drive, Susie began to relate some of her suspicions about Becky and Bobby, but they were so terrible that Nancy hardly knew what to believe. Becky had been telling Nancy and the other members of the family for some time that Susie was suffering from dementia, so she did not know if what she was hearing was true, or just the result of an illness her mother might be suffering from.

Susie asked Nancy to take her to the The First State Bank and Trust so that she could take out some emergency cash in case things got worse at home. Nancy agreed to do so, and helped her mother into the bank.

However, when they spoke with a teller, Susie was informed that her bank account had been closed. Shocked, she asked for the key to her safe deposit box. What she found inside it devastated her beyond words. Other than a few personal papers, the box was empty. All of the money that Susie and Aldon had saved during their lives was gone, as was the deed to her home.

Nancy led Susie, who was trembling and crying, out of the bank. She tried to comfort her, but had no answers other than to offer to take her to see a lawyer. Nancy had been with Susie in the past when she had accessed her safe deposit box, and knew that it had at one time been full of money, even though she did not know the exact amount. So she believed at least that part of Susie's story was true.

When they arrived back at the trailer, Nancy wanted to go inside with her mother, but Susie said she wanted to confront Becky herself. She promised to call Nancy if she needed her, and went in.

Becky was waiting just inside the

door, watching as her mother came up the walk. As soon as she closed the door behind her, Susie accused Becky of having taken her money and demanded that she give it back and get out of her house. A terrible argument raged all evening, until Susie began having heart palpitations and feeling faint.

Becky helped Susie into bed, where she remained for several days, depressed and hopeless. But as her strength returned, Susie again began demanding that her daughter return her money and leave her home.

On November 11, Becky drove Susie to the Appalachian Regional Hospital in

Beckley for a scheduled cancer appointment. While Susie was being examined by her oncologist, Becky made arrangements for Susie to once again be admitted to the psychiatric ward, saying that her mother was delusional and threatening.

Susie was distraught at having to be put into a locked room on the psychiatric floor again, when all she wanted to do was to go home and be with Patsy. When the doctor questioned her about Becky's accusations that she was delusional, homicidal and suicidal, Susie denied them and told the doctor that her daughter and son-in-law were stealing from her and that they had taken money from her purse and from her safe deposit box at the bank.

In his report, Dr. Faheem wrote *"This is a 74 year old white female, who was brought in by her family. The patient was coming here today to get tested because of a lung mass we found at her last admission. The patient's daughter thought it would be best for her to be admitted to the Psychiatric Unit. The patient has been delusional lately. She has become threatening towards her daughter and son-in-law, accusing them of stealing from her, and other things that the* *patient's daughter states are just delusions. The patient states that during her last admission, $100,000 was stolen out of her safety deposit box and states that $1,300.00 in cash out of her pocketbook has been taken over the last couple of months."*

Susie remained at the hospital for three days for observation, but was found to be competent and not a danger to herself or anyone else, and was sent home with Becky, who was furious that her mother had not been kept in the hospital psychiatric ward.

Becky warned Susie that the next time she caused any problems she would be put into a mental institution for the rest of her

life, and that she would never be allowed to

return home or see her daughter Patsy again.

CHAPTER FOUR

During the two weeks following her hospital stay, Susie did not cause any problems for Becky or Bobby. She sat quietly in her chair during the day and went to bed early each night. She ate very little, only what few items she could be sure had not been tampered with.

Susie noticed that while she was in the hospital, a new phone had replaced the one that had always sat on the living room table. Becky told her that the old one had stopped working, so they bought a new speed dial telephone for her.

Susie sometimes had trouble seeing the numbers on the old phone, and this one had large buttons, and all of her frequently called numbers had been programmed in so that she only had to push one button to reach the person whose name was written beside it.

Susie's daughter Nancy was number 1 on the phone, but although Susie tried several times to call her when Becky and Bobby were out of the room, she always got a busy signal. The same thing was true for her daughter Connie's number, and for her grand daughter Tammy Workman's number. Everyone, it seemed, was too busy to answer Susie's calls, or to call and check in on her.

The Thanksgiving holiday came and went without incident, but on the 28th of November, a serious disagreement erupted because Susie did not want Bobby helping to bathe Patsy or take her to the bathroom. She felt that it was not proper for a man to do such personal things with her daughter. The fight ended when Becky stormed out of the house, vowing that Susie would be sorry.

Susie was so exhausted that she went to her room and lay down. She began to pray, asking God to help her and her daughter Patsy. Suddenly, she felt a sense of peace envelope her. Later, she described the feeling

as 'the peace that passes all understanding'

from one of her favorite Bible verses, and she

fell into a deep sleep.

Meanwhile, Becky had left the trailer

and gone to the Greenbrier County Circuit

Court in Lewisburg where she filed a Mental

Hygiene Warrant against Susie. A Mental

Hygiene Warrant authorizes law enforcement

to take a person into custody who shows

symptoms of immediate and serious need for

help for a mental illness, or who are at

immediate and serious risk of harming

themselves or others. The warrant orders a

person to undergo a mental health evaluation by a doctor to determine if they should be involuntarily placed in a mental institution.

Becky filled out a warrant against her mother at the courthouse, stating that Susie was mentally ill. She also swore that Susie was in danger of killing herself or someone else. Becky wrote that Susie had already been admitted twice to the psychiatric ward of the Appalachian Regional Hospital for observation, using that information as proof that Susie was insane, although she did not mention that on both occasions Susie was found to be competent and had been released.

After filling out the warrant against Susie, by law Becky was required to sign a notarized document, stating that *"I further certify, UNDER PENALTIES OF FALSE SWEARING as provided for by law, that the information, statements and allegations contained in this Petition and Application are true and accurate to the best of my knowledge, information and belief and constitute the sole basis and reason for the making of this application.*

I understand that if I knowingly provide FALSE information on this application, I could be subject to a criminal charge of false swearing, and possibly liable

for civil damages." After signing the

statement she knew to be a lie, Becky

returned home to wait for the warrant to be

served on her unsuspecting mother.

Susie woke from her sleep, still feeling

calm and at peace, and took her Bible with

her to the living room, where she sat in her

recliner next to Patsy's chair, and read out

loud to her handicapped daughter.

Susie noticed that Becky and Bobby

seemed excited and nervous. They brought

her coffee and soda several times and tried to

make her drink them, but she ignored them

and concentrated on her reading.

At 4:30, there was a loud knock on the front door, and Becky ran to answer it. A tall, imposing Deputy from the Greenbrier County Sheriff's office entered the room, and told Susie that he had a warrant for her arrest. Susie was so shocked and frightened that all the strength left her body and she was unable to move. She had no idea of what was happening, and began to cry helplessly.

The officer assisted her to her feet and handcuffed the tiny 74 year old woman, who only weighed 90 pound and was suffering from cancer and liver disease, and led her towards the door.

Patsy became very upset when she saw that the her mother was crying and being taken away by the policeman. She struggled to get up from her chair and follow them, calling "Mommy, Mommy." Susie looked back over her shoulder and said "Its all right Patsy, Mommy will be home soon. Mommy loves you."

The officer took Susie out to his police cruiser, where she was placed in the back seat of the car. The last thing she saw as she was driven away was Becky glaring at her through the bars of the police car window.

To her shame, several neighbors witnessed her arrest, making Susie feel like a criminal even though she had never broken the law in her entire life.

The drive to the County Sheriff's Office seemed to take an eternity, and Susie's mouth was so dry that she could not speak. She felt the fear and hysteria within her bubbling up, threatening to overcome her. But she knew that if she lost control, she would appear to be unstable, which was what Becky was hoping would happen. Instead, Susie began repeating to herself "Yea, though I walk through the Valley of the Shadow of

Death, I will fear no Evil, for Thou art With Me." She felt her pounding heart slow down and a feeling of calm washed over her. Finally, the cruiser pulled into the parking lot of the Sheriff's Office, and Susie was led inside.

The WV Seneca Mental Health Department had been notified of the hearing, and had appointed attorney Eric M. Francis to represent Susie as her counsel. The Mental Health Commissioner, Douglas Arbuckle, had arranged for licenced Psychologist Beverly McBride to evaluate Susie and determine if she needed to be involuntarily committed to a mental facility.

Susie was taken into a room with Ms. McBride, and they talked for what seemed like hours to Susie. Ms. McBride appeared to be a kind and compassionate woman, and Susie poured her heart out to her, telling her about all of the abuse she had suffered. Susie revealed how everything that made her life of any value had been stripped from her, her home, her money, her pride, her dignity and her hope. Susie exhibited no trace of a mental illness, only sorrow and a weary determination to overcome her desperate situation.

Eventually, Susie was asked to perform various tests to show that she was competent and not dangerous. At the end of the evaluation, Ms. McBride's findings stated that there was no probable cause to believe that Susie was mentally ill, and that the accusations brought against her were not warranted.

Becky was brought in and intensively questioned during the hearing, and she finally admitted that both she and her husband Bobby had been giving Susie double doses of her anti-depressant medications (Zoloft and Xanax) in an effort to 'calm her'- actions that could possibly be prosecuted as criminal.

Ms. McBride's final evaluation was that the family needed therapy mediation, and she released Susie and told Becky to drive her mother home.

Becky was disgusted that Susie had not been placed in a mental institution, and they did not speak on the long drive back to Quinwood. When they arrived at the trailer, an administrator from the Seneca Mental Health / Mental Retardation Council (which provided services for Patsy) was waiting to speak with Susie and Becky about the incident.

Susie was by that time feeling very
weak and ill, and begged someone to call her
daughter Nancy. Becky called her at the
administrator's request and a few minutes
later Nancy arrived at the trailer. She sat
down and the situation was explained to her
by the Seneca administrator.

Aghast at what Susie had been put
through, Nancy told the administrator that she
believed Becky and Bobby were abusing her
mother. Nancy said that Susie was competent
to handle her own affairs and to care for
Patsy, and she wanted Becky and Bobby to
move out of her home.

After a long discussion, it was decided that Becky and Bobby would resign from their positions with the Seneca program immediately, and leave Susie's trailer at once. The couple quickly gathered their personal belongings and left.

Nancy agreed to spend the night at the trailer, and to drive Susie to the magistrate's office the following day to find out what legal resources were available to have her stolen belongings restored to her.

After Becky and her husband had departed, Nancy asked her mother why she had not called her when the police came to arrest her, to which Susie replied that she could never reach anyone because the phone lines were always busy.

Nancy said that her phone was hardly ever in use, and when she and the Seneca administrator checked Susie's phone, they found that all the numbers on the speed dial were programmed to call Susie's own number, which meant she would get a busy signal when she tried to call any member of her family. Both women were appalled at the level of abuse Susie had been subjected to by her own daughter.

Before taking her leave, the Seneca

administrator made plans for Susie to sign papers showing that she, as a competent adult, would now be working with Seneca as Patsy's guardian, and arranged for two new Seneca workers to be assigned to Patsy's case.

After Nancy and Patsy retired for the night, Susie knelt down and thanked God for delivering her from her torment, then got into her bed feeling safe and secure for first time since her long ordeal began.

CHAPTER FIVE

On the morning of November 29th,
Susie woke with a terrible feeling of anxiety.
Then she remembered that Becky and Bobby
were gone and that Nancy was in the trailer
with her, and she relaxed, happy to be free.

Nancy fixed a good breakfast for her
mother and sister, and then called Connie,
Susie's second youngest daughter who lived
in Rupert, and asked her to meet them at the
magistrate's office that morning.

Nancy helped Patsy and Susie to the
car, and drove them the short distance to the
nearby town. Connie, a petite and pretty

brunette, had notified her supervisor at the

Greenbrier Resort where she worked that she

needed the day off, and was waiting for them

in the parking lot. They greeted each other

and went into the building, which housed both

the magistrate's office and the Greenbrier

County Sheriff's office.

When it was time for Susie to meet

with the magistrate, she explained to him that

two of her children, Becky Jones and David

George, had taken her money and her

property, and asked him what she needed to

do to get it back. The magistrate picked up

the phone and called Barry Bruce, a well

known and respected attorney in Lewisburg, and made an appointment for Susie with him for that day. He also advised Susie to think about filing theft charges against Becky and David after she consulted with the attorney.

Nancy, Connie, Susie and Patsy drove straight to the lawyers office, where they met with Mr. Bruce. After hearing Susie's story, he advised her to make a new will and a new power of attorney, and had her fill out papers revoking David and Becky's power of attorney over her.

Mr. Bruce instructed his secretary to take down Susie's information so that her new will and power of attorney could be

drawn up, and requested that Susie come

back in a few days to sign them. Mr. Bruce

also asked her to provide him with mailing

addresses for Becky and David, so that his

office could contact them and start

proceedings to recover everything they had

stolen from her. Susie agreed, then had

Nancy drive her and Patsy back to their empty

and peaceful trailer. Connie and Nancy both

checked in on them often over the next few

days, but it was soon apparent that Susie was

more than capable of taking care of herself

and Patsy, as well as the housework and

cooking, and that they were both very happy

being on their own. Soon, the two new

employees from Seneca began coming to the

trailer eight hours each day to help with

Patsy. They were friendly and sweet, and

Susie quickly became fond of them both,

calling them 'her girls.'

Nancy and Connie returned with Susie

and Patsy to Barry Bruce's office on the 9th

of December, and Susie signed a Revocation

of Power of Authority against Becky and

David. She also signed a new will naming

Nancy and Connie as her Executrixes and as

Guardians of her daughter Patsy in the event

of her death. Additionally, she signed a new

Power of Authority for Nancy and Connie, to

be used if she should become incapacitated.

Susie gave her approval to a letter that Mr.

Bruce had prepared to send to David and to

Becky. The letter read:

SUBJECT:

SUSIE GEORGE AND PATSY GEORGE

Dear Ms. Jones and Mr. George:

This law firm represents the above subject in

regard to various matters, including the

properties of her estate and revocations of

certain powers of attorney.

Enclosed for your information and records is

a Revocation of Power of Attorney wherein

Ms. George has elected to revoke that certain

power of attorney naming you as her joint

attorneys in fact. This document has been

placed on record in the *Office of the Clerk of*

the County Commission in Book 15 at page

224, and the power of attorney given to you

is now null and void.

We have also obtained a copy of the Power

of Attorney given to you by Patsy George on

or about Feb. 7, 1997. Enclosed is a

Voluntary Revocation of that Power of

Attorney which we would appreciate your

signing before a Notary Public and returning

to us promptly for recording. As you are

aware, Patsy is an incapacitated,

incompetent person and is unable to legally

execute a Power of Attorney. It is not our

desire to file a legal action to have the Power

of Attorney revoked; however, we will have

no alternative if you elect not to sign the

enclosed Voluntary Revocation.

We are also Enclosing a Deed for your

signature before a Notary Public. By signing

this Deed, you are conveying all your right,

title and interest in and to Ms. George's

property to her, where it rightfully belongs.

Likewise, it is not our desire to file any legal

action to obtain possession of the property on

behalf of Ms. George; however if the deed is

not executed by you, then we will have no

other alternative. We look forward to your

prompt cooperation and return of these

signed, notarized documents. Thank you.

Within several weeks of the letters

being mailed, both Becky and David returned

Susie's property and money, and sent signed

copies of their revocations for their power of

attorneys of Patsy and Susie to Barry Bruce.

For the remainder of her life, Susie

stayed in her home with her daughter Patsy,

caring for her with the help of the Seneca

Mental Health Council employees. Susie's daughters Nancy and Connie were happy to drive her and Patsy whenever they needed to go out, and helped their mother learn to manage her finances.

Susie's mental competence was never called into question again, and she and Patsy were able to resume the lives they had been living before Susie became a victim of elder abuse.

EPILOGUE

The number one reason that elder abuse goes unreported in America is that, in ninety per cent of the cases, it is perpetrated by a close family member. The victims do not file charges against their abusers because they still love them, or because they do not want others to know that they have been mistreated by a relative.

Although she was urged to do so by family members and by many of the residents of Quinwood, including a former police officer, Susie George decided not to press criminal charges against Becky or David for stealing her money and property, or against

Becky for filing a false warrant in an effort to

have her confined to a mental institution. She

still loved them both and prayed that God

would forgive them for their heinous acts.

Susie believed that the legal steps she

had taken in making a new will and a new

power of attorney were enough to prevent

David or Becky from ever harming her or

Patsy again. But because there were never

any official charges filed, that was not the

case.

Susie passed away in March of 1998.

It was her final wish that Connie Bennett be

named as Patsy's legal guardian. After her
funeral, Connie met with her siblings Mary
Holloway, Becky Jones, and David George to
discuss the will and Patsy's guardianship.

Becky, David and Mary agreed to a
settlement wherein they would each receive a
sum of $5000.00, for which in return they
would honor Susie's wishes and would not
interfere with the will being probated or with
Connie being named guardian for Patsy.
Connie wrote each of them a check, which
they accepted and cashed.

However, when Connie filed for legal
guardianship of Patsy several months later,

Becky Jones entered a counter claim for guardianship, breaking her agreement with Connie in doing so.

Because Susie had never filed criminal or civil charges against Becky, Connie could not produce any legal documents at the hearing that would have called into question Becky's claim that she was qualified to be a guardian. Therefore, as is common in cases where there are two family members seeking guardianship, the Mental Health Commissioner tried to reach a compromise by appointing Connie as Patsy's guardian as specified in Susie's will, and then by making Becky one of the Trustees of Patsy's finances.

Connie, knowing that such an arrangement would not be in accordance with her mother's wishes, refused to abide by the court order. She did not realize that her actions would mean that she was in contempt of court.

A new hearing was scheduled, and because of her non-compliance with the court order, Connie was removed as guardian, and in what I believe to be a terrible miscarriage of justice, the court named Becky as Patsy George's conservator.

I included this information in my
book in order to impress on victims of elder
abuse that no matter what their relationship is
to someone, the authorities should be notified
and civil or criminal charges should be filed
against the perpetrators of the offense.
Otherwise, they will be free to repeat their
abuse on other victims in the future.

APPENDIX

Documentation for Incidents in This Book

1. Power of Attorney - Susie George to Becky and David

2. Deed for Aldon, Susie and Patsy George

3. Illegal Power of Attorney - Patsy George to Becky and David

4. Withdrawal of Funds by Becky Jones

5. Psychiatric Report from ARH : 8-18-97

6. Psychiatric Report from ARH : 11-11-97

7. Mental Hygiene Warrant - Case # 97-MH-48

8. Revoked Power of Attorney -Susie George to Becky and David

9. Revoked Power of Attorney -Patsy George from Becky

10. New Will of Susie George

11. New Power of Attorney for Susie George

12. Letter from Barry Bruce to Becky and David

13. Cancelled Settlement Checks from Becky, David and Mary

14. Connie Bennett removed as Guardian

91

FEE:$3.50   Ret.To; Rebecca Jones
P.O. Box 44
Quinwood,WV 25981

POWER OF ATTORNEY

KNOW ALL MEN BY THESE PRESENTS: That I, SUSIE GEORGE of Greenbrier County, West Virginia, have made, constituted and appointed, and by these presents do make, constitute and appoint my daughter, REBECCA JONES and/or my son, DAVID GEORGE, my true and lawful attorneys for me and in my name, place and stead, and for my use and benefit, to ask, demand, sue for, recover, collect and receive all such sums of money, debts, dues, accounts, interest, dividends and demands whatsoever as are now, or shall hereafter become due, owing, payable or belonging to me, and have, use and

Document 1-Page 1

93

take all lawful ways and means in my name or otherwise for the recover thereof, and to compromise and agree for the same, execute sufficient discharges for the same, for me and in my name, place and stead, to bargain, contract, argue for, purchase, receive, and take lands, tenements, hereditaments, and accept the seizing and possession of all lands and all deeds and other assurances therefore, and to lease, let, demise, bargain, sell, remise, release, convey, mortgage and hypothecate lands, tenements and hereditaments upon such terms and conditions and under such covenants as they shall think for. Also, to bargain and agree for, buy, sell, mortgage, hypothecate and in any way and manner deal in and with goods, wares, and merchandise, choses in action and other property in possession or in action, and to make, do and transact all and every kind of business of what nature or kind soever, and also for me and my name, and as my act and deed, to sign, seal,

BOOK **14** PAGE **619**

Document 1-Page 2

execute, deliver and acknowledge such deeds, leases and assignment of leases, covenants, indentures, agreements, mortgages, bonds, notes, receipts, evidence of debts, releases and satisfaction of mortgage judgements and other debts, and such other instruments in writing of whatever kind and nature as may be necessary or proper in the premises.

Giving and granting unto my said attorneys full power and authority to do and perform all and every act and thing whatsoever requisite and necessary to be done in and about the premises, as fully to all intents and purposes as I might or could do if personally present, with full power of substitution or revocation, hereby ratifying and confirming all that my said attorneys, or their substitute shall lawfully do or cause to be done by virtue of these presents. It is the intention that this Power of Attorney shall survive the incapacitation, including incompetency, if any, of the undersigned.

WITNESS my hand this _19th_ day of January, 1997.

_____
SUSIE GEORGE

Document 1-Page 3

95

MAR 13 1981

Mailed to Aldon George
           Box 93
Fee $1.75   Quinwood W. Va. 29581

THIS DEED, made this the 12th day of December, 1979, by and between ALDON GEORGE, husband of Susie George, hereinafter called the party of the first part, and SUSIE GEORGE, wife of Aldon George, and PATSY SUE GEORGE, daughter of Aldon George, hereinafter called the parties of the second part:

W I T N E S S E T H:

THAT for and in consideration of the sum of Ten ($10.00) Dollars, cash in hand paid, the receipt of which is hereby acknowleged, the said party of the first part has remised, released and forever quitted claim and by these presents do remise, release and forever quit claim unto the said parties of the second part, all of his right, title and interest whatsoever in and to the following described property, to wit;

Document 2-Page 1

97

All of the surface of, but including no minerals or
mineral rights in, the following described lots or parcels
of land situate in Meadow Bluff Tax District, Western
Magisterial District, Greenbrier County, West Virginia,

Lot No. 20, in Block C, fronting 40 feet on Church Street
and extending back by parallel lines 100 feet to an alley
and adjoining Lot No. 19 in Block C, all as designated and
shown on the Revised Map of the Town of Quinwood, bearing
date April 1, 1925, of the division thereof into lots, streets
and alleys by W. E. R. Byrne, Trustee, which Revised Map
is of record in the office of the Clerk of Greenbrier
County Court, and reference to which is here made for a
more particular description and location of the premises
hereby conveyed.

Lots 18 and 19, Block "C" as laid down, described, and
shown on the revised map of the Town of Quinwood, bearing
date April 1, 1925, and recorded in the office of the
Clerk of the County Court of said County of Greenbrier.

AND being a part of the same real estate acquired by Aldon

George and Sussie George, from Adrian G. Douglas and Irene

Douglas, his wife, by deed dated May 22, 1973 and of record

in the office of the Clerk of Greenbrier County, West Virginia,

in Deed Book 279 at page 172.

Sussie George, wife of Aldon George and Susie George are

Document 2-Page 2

one and the same person.

THE Grantor herein, Aldon George, does hereby expressly reserve a life estate in the aforementioned property to himself, which includes the unrestricted, exclusive, and full right to use, occupy, rent or lease the subject property during his lifetime.

REFERENCE is hereby made to all prior deeds for a more particular and complete description of said property and of any reservations, restrictions and exceptions and for all pertinent purposes.

DECLARATION OF CONSIDERATION OF VALUE

Under the penalties of fine and imprisonment as provided by law, we hereby declare the total consideration paid for the property conveyed by the document to which this declaration is appended is $100.00.

WITNESS the following signature and seal.

Aldon George (SEAL)

ALDON GEORGE

Document 2-Page 3

STATE OF WEST VIRGINIA

COUNTY OF GREENBRIER TO WIT:

I, _C. Thos. Bobbitt_ a Notary Public in and

for the county and state aforesaid, do hereby certify that ALDON

GEORGE, husband of Susie George, whose name is signed to the

document above bearing date of the 12th of December, 1979, has

this day acknowledged the same before me in my said county.

Given under my hand this 19 day of Dec ,

19 79 . My commission expires January 5 1986

Notary Public

This instrument was prepared by C. Thomas Bobbitt,
Attorney at Law, 132 N. Court St., Lewisburg, WV

WEST VIRGINIA, Greenbrier County, S. S:
In the Clerk's Office of Greenbrier County Court 4th day of March 1981
This DEED was this day presented in the office aforesaid and thereupon, together with the
Certificate thereto annexed, admitted to record.
Teste _Eugene V. Perry_ Clerk
By _____ Deputy

Document 2-Page 4

100

FEE:$3.50   Ret.To; J. Michael Anderson

POWER OF ATTORNEY

KNOW ALL MEN BY THESE PRESENTS: That I, PATSY S. GEORGE, of Greenbrier County, West Virginia, have made, constituted and appointed, and by these presents do make, constitute and appoint my sister, REBECCA JONES and/or my brother, DAVID GEORGE my true and lawful attorneys for me and in my name, place and stead, and for my use and benefit, to ask, demand, sue for, recover, collect and receive all such sums of money, debts, dues, accounts, interest, dividends and demands whatsoever as are now, or shall hereafter become due, owing, payable or belonging to me, and have, use and take all lawful ways and means in my name or otherwise for the recover thereof, and to compromise and agree for the same, execute sufficient discharges for the same, for me and in my name, place and stead, to bargain, contract, argue for, purchase, receive, and take lands, tenements, hereditaments, and accept the seizing and possession of all lands and all deeds and other assurances therefore, and to lease, let, demise, bargain, sell, remise, release, convey, mortgage and hypothecate lands, tenements and hereditaments upon such terms and conditions and under such covenants as they shall think for. Also, to bargain and agree for, buy, sell, mortgage, hypothecate and in any way and manner deal in and with goods, wares, and merchandise, choses in action and other property in possession or in action, and to make, do and transact all and every kind of business of what nature or kind soever, and also for me and my name, and as my act and deed, to sign, seal,

BOOK **14** PAGE **763**

Document 3-Page 1

101

execute, deliver and acknowledge such deeds, leases and assignment of leases, covenants, indentures, agreements, mortgages, bonds, notes, receipts, evidence of debts, releases and satisfaction of mortgage judgements and other debts, and such other instruments in writing of whatever kind and nature as may be necessary or proper in the premises.

Giving and granting unto my said attorneys full power and authority to do and perform all and every act and thing whatsoever requisite and necessary to be done in and about the premises, as fully to all intents and purposes as I might or could do if personally present, with full power of substitution or revocation, hereby ratifying and confirming all that my said attorneys, or their substitute shall lawfully do or cause to be done by virtue of these presents. It is the intention that this Power of Attorney shall survive the incapacitation, including incompetency, if any, of the undersigned.

WITNESS my hand this ___7th___ day of ___February___, 1997.

_____
PATSY S. GEORGE

Document 3-Page 2

102

STATE OF WEST VIRGINIA

COUNTY OF GREENBRIER, TO-WIT:

I, ___Debra E. O'Dell___ , a Notary Public in and for the County and State aforesaid, do certify that PATSY S. GEORGE whose name is signed to the writing above, bearing date the ___7th___ day of ___February___, 1997, has this day acknowledged the same before me.

Given under my hand and Official Notarial Seal this 7th day of ___February___, 1997.

My commission expires ___September 30, 1997___.

S E A L

_____
Notary Public

THIS DOCUMENT PREPARED BY:
J. Michael Anderson, Attorney at Law
702 Main Street
Rainelle, West Virginia 25962

BOOK 14 PAGE 765

Document 3-Page 3

103

FIRST STATE BANK & TRUST

Fri Jan 29, 1999

ACCOUNT NO.   704849

Research Item Copy

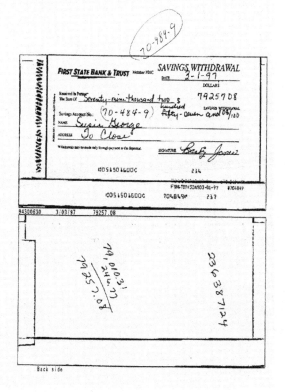

FIRST STATE BANK & TRUST Member FDIC

SAVINGS WITHDRAWAL

DATE 3-1-97

70-489-9

Received in Payment
The Sum Of *Seventy-nine-thousand two* $ 7925708
hundred
fifty- seven and 08/100

Savings Account No.: (70-484-9)

NAME *Susie George*

ADDRESS *To Close*

Withdrawals may be made only through payment to the depositor.

SIGNATURE *Betsy James*

⑈05150⑈600⑈   234

⑈05150⑈600⑈   704849⑈   237

FSB4-709492A403-01-97   #704849

94300630   3/03/97   79257.08

79,010.31
79257.08
80.00?

2363871P4

Back side

Document 4

HISTORY AND PHYSICAL EXAMINATION

Patient: **GEORGE, SUSIE**		Patient #: **007424**
Attending Physician: AHMED D. FAHEEM, M. D.		
Service: PSYCHIATRY	Location: **166**	
Admission Date: 08-18-97		
Dictation Date: 08-19-97 @ 1630	Transcription Date: 08-20-97 @ 1345	

HISTORY: This is a 74-year old female who was admitted with severe depression and homicidal ideations. The patient has been extremely depressed and has been expressing significant hopeless, helpless, and despondent feelings, feels very frustrated because she states she has been having more and more difficulty in taking care of her mentally retarded 49-year old daughter. The patient also states that she is also having stressors due to her other children. Her husband died and her other daughter and son-in-law have come in and are trying to make major changes in the family. The patient has been rather suspicious, distrustful, and paranoid and reportedly has threatened to kill the daughter and son-in-law or told them that she had a gun. The patient says that she does not recall doing so and feels upset and frustrated over her situation. However, the rest of the details are as dictated by Connie England.

MENTAL STATUS EXAMINATION; She is tense, anxious, edgy, depressed, rather suspicious, guarded, oriented for place, person, year. She had some difficulty with date and time. Attention and concentration is impaired. She had difficulty with mental calculations and serial sevens. She is able to give the days of the week in reverse order. Her memory and recall for recent events was slightly impaired. She was able to recall one out of three objects after five minutes. Judgment was intact. There is no evidence of any looseness of association, flight of ideation, or push of speech. Fund of knowledge was appropriate for her educational level and background. She denied being actively suicidal or homicidal.

DIAGNOSTIC IMPRESSION:

AXIS I:
1) Major affective illness (depression).
AXIS II:
No diagnosis.
AXIS III:
1) High blood pressure.
2) Chronic arthritis.
3) Liver disease.
AXIS IV:
1) Moderately severe.

Document 5

APPALACHIAN REGIONAL HEALTHCARE, INC.
Beckley-ARH Hospital
306 Stanaford Road
Beckley, West Virginia 25801

HISTORY AND PHYSICAL EXAMINATION

Patient: **GEORGE, SUSIE ELIZABETH**	Patient #: **007424**
Attending Physician: AHMED D. FAHEEM, M. D.	
Service: PSYCHIATRY	Location: 166-1
Admission Date: 11/11/97	
Dictation Date: 11/11/97 @ 1534	Transcription Date: 11/11/97 @ 1833

HISTORY OF PRESENT ILLNESS: This is a 74-year-old white female,
who was brought in by her family. The patient was coming here today
to get tested because of a lung mass that was found on her last
admission. The patient's Daughter thought it would be best for her to
be admitted to the Psychiatric Unit. The patient has been delusional
lately. She has become threatening towards her Daughter and Son-in-
law, accusing them of stealing from her and other things that the
patient's Daughter states are just delusions. The patient states
during her last admission, $100,000 was stolen out of her safety
deposit box and states that $1,300 in cash out of her pocketbook has
been taken over the last couple of months. The patient also admits to
being depressed lately. She has been withdrawing. She has not wanted
to eat anything. She has just been wanting to sit around. She has
been worrying constantly. She states that she thinks she may have
cancer or TB and is wanting to find out the results of the test coming
up. Also, her 51-year-old mentally retarded Daughter recently had a
stroke, and she has been worried about her. She says that she is very
concerned about her and worries about her constantly. The patient
denies any suicidal or homicidal ideations but just states she has
been depressed, and it is getting hard for her to do things. Her
Daughter was very concerned and noticed that the patient has been
getting more and more delusional and depressed. Therefore, she was
admitted to the hospital.

PAST MEDICAL HISTORY: The patient has a lung mass, which is
due to have biopsy on Friday. She has arthritis, hypertension,
history of liver disease.

ALLERGIES: Alcohol and Iodine.

FAMILY HISTORY: The patient was raised in Greenbrier
County by her Mom and Dad. Her Mom and Dad have been dead for many
years. Her Mom died in her 80s of old age complications. Her Dad
died from an MI at age 64. The patient has 8 brothers and 2 sisters.
Only she, one Brother and one Sister are living.

SOCIAL HISTORY: The patient was married once for 40
years. She says her Husband died about 18 years ago from black lung.

Document 6

109

Mental Hygiene Warrant
against Susie E George of Box 93, Quinwood,WV 25981
Alleged abuse of daughter
Filed by Becky Jones of Box 44, Quinwood, WV 25981
Delivered and Carried out by Greenbrier County Deputy Frankie
On November 28, 1997
Heard by Beverly McBride for Mental Hygiene Commissioner Douglas Arbuckle

Document 7-Page 1

111

IN THE CIRCUIT COURT OF _Greenbrier_ COUNTY, WEST VIRGINIA

IN RE: Involuntary Hospitalization of

Case No. _97-MH-48_

Susie E. George
RESPONDENT

ORDER:
FOR DETENTION, PROBABLE CAUSE HEARING, AND EXAMINATION
[W.Va. Code §27-5-2(b)(4)]

On the _28th_ day of _November, 1997_ _____

Janice Rebecca Jones _____, made application to this Court to order

Susie P. George _____ be taken into custody and detained for the purpose of a probable cause
(Respondent's Name)
hearing and for the purpose of examination of the Respondent by a physician or psychologist, pursuant to the provisions of West

Virginia Code §27-5-2(b)(4).

This Court FINDS the application sets forth facts which are sufficient to meet the requirements for detention, custody, and

examination as provided by W.Va. Code §27-5-2(a).

Accordingly, it is ORDERED that the Sheriff of this County take into custody, detain, and bring the Respondent before this

Court on the _28th_ day of _November, 1997_, at the hour of _4:30_ p. m., at which time the probable cause

hearing will be conducted.

It is further ORDERED that the attorney named below is appointed as counsel to represent the Respondent in this matter.

Name of Appointed Attorney: _Eric M. Francis_

Attorney's Address: _203 Green Lane_

Lewisburg, WV 24901

Attorney's Telephone No.: _( ) 647-3058_

It is further ORDERED that the _Seneca_ mental health facility provide or arrange for an

examination of the Respondent by a physician or psychologist as required by law prior to the probable cause hearing and report

thereon to the Court at the hearing as scheduled above. [See W.Va. Code §27-5-2(b)(4).]

The Clerk shall enter this Order as of the date first above written and transmit an attested copy thereof to the Sheriff of this

County, to the _Seneca_ mental health facility, to appointed counsel

named above, and to the Prosecuting Attorney of _Greenbrier_ County, West Virginia.

Douglas H. Abdell

MENTAL HYGIENE COMMISSIONER / JUDGE

SCA-MH 903CC / 10-92

FILED DEC 1 1997

RONALD F. MILLER, Clerk

Document 7-Page 2

112

IN RE: INVOLUNTARY HOSPITALIZATION OF _Susie E. George_

RESPONDANT

DATE: _11/28/97_   CASE NO: _97-MH-48_

If this application is GRANTED, distribute copies of the application and Grant Order to: Applicant; Respondant; Respondant's Attorney; Prosecuting Attorney; and Seneca Mental Health.

If this application is DENIED, file the application with the Denial Order and provide the Applicant with copies of the application and the Denial Order.

APPLICATION FOR INVOLUNTARY CUSTODY FOR MENTAL HEALTH EXAMINATION
(W. Va. CODE SECTION 27-5-2)

INSTRUCTIONS TO APPLICANT:

A. All information must be printed or typed and be clearly readable.

B. All information requested must be provided, if known. If unknown, you must state that it is unknown.

C. Any petition and application which does not provide the necessary information, or is unreadable, may be rejected or denied. Read and answer all questions carefully.

D. In this document, the RESPONDANT is the person whose examanation is requested.

---

1. Applicant's full name: _Janice Rebecca Jones_
2. Applicant's full mailing address: _PO Box 44_
   Quinwood, WV 25981
   Telephone Number: Work: ( ) _438-8429_ Home: ( ) _438-8618_
3. Full name of Respondant: _Susie Elizabeth George_
4. Respondant's last known address: _PO Box 93_
   Quinwood, WV 25981
5. Where is Respondant now? _As above_

---

6. Is the Respondant a resident of this county? _✓_ YES _____ NO
7. Is the Respondant currently present in this county? _✓_ YES _____ NO
8. What is your relationship to the Respondant? _daughter_

Document 7-Page 3
113

9. Respondent's spouse's name, address and telephone number: widowed

10. Respondent's parents or guardians' names, addresses and telephone numbers: deceased

11. Respondent's next of kin's name, address, telephone number and relation to Respondent Janice Jones, PO Box 44, Quinwood WV 438-8618

12. (a). Do you believe the Respondent is addicted to drugs and/or alcohol? NO
    (b). Do you believe the Respondent is mentally ill? yes
    (c). Do you believe the Respondent is mentally retarded? NO

13. What behavior of the Respondent have you personally observed upon which to base your opinion? last night threatned to take medication to kill self, has not been sleeping, running up and down halls singing, is threating to kill new person who will be in her home to care for MR daughter, has cancer and says god has cured her + is not going back

14. How long has the Respondent shown such behavior? since thanksgiving morn. to Dr.

15. (a). Do you believe as a result that the Respondent is likely to cause serious harm to him/her self? it's a possibility if she does not receive immediate treatmen
    (b). Do you believe as a result that the Respondent is likely to cause serious harm to others? Yes

16. What specific acts by the Respondent have you personally observed within the past 72 hours upon which you base your opinion? verbally abusive, excessive energy, up all night, sudden episodes of crying, accusing family of stealing, threatened to take pill to be with dead husband, hopes that God will take her, cleaning house at night

17. List the names and addresses of any other persons who have observed such behavior by the Respondent within the past 72 hours. Bobby Jones; PO Box 44, Quinwood WV Bobby Jones III, as above

18. Has the Respondent been under the care of a Physician? Dr. Patricia Henderson
    If so, Physician's name and address: Allegheny Regional Hosp.

19. Has the Respondent been examined by a Psychiatrist or Psychologist? BAR-H
    If so, please provide the name and address: BAR-H, Dr. Faheem and Gary Keesee counselor

20. Please provide the names, addresses and time periods for any hospitals in which the Respondent has been confined for any period of time for reasons of mental illness, mental retardation and/or addiction to alcohol/drugs: Bar-H 2 wks. ago, BAR-H in Aug.

Document 7-Page 4

114

STATE OF WEST VIRGINIA,

COUNTY OF GREENBRIER, to-wit:

I, __Janice Rebecca Jones__ , the Applicant and Petitioner named herein, do hereby certify that I have reason to believe that __Susie Elizabeth George__ is __✓__ mentally ill, _____ mentally retarded and/or _____ addicted to either alcohol or drugs, and because of such condition is likely to cause serious harm to him/her self and/or others if allowed to remain at liberty, and should therefore be committed for care and treatment.

I therefore petition that the Respondent be brought before the Court in order that the Court may determine what further actions, if any, are warranted according to the provisions of the West Virginia Code.

I further certify, UNDER PENALTIES OF FALSE SWEARING as provided for by law, that the information, statements and allegations contained in this Petition and Application are true and accurate to the best of my knowledge, information and belief and consitute the sole basis and reasons for the making of this application.

I understand that if I knowingly provide FALSE information in this application, I could be subject to a criminal charge of false swearing, and possibly liable for civil damages.

DATE: __11-28-97__   _Janice Rebecca Jones_
                                          APPLICANT'S SIGNATURE

TAKEN, subscribed and sworn to before me, the undersigned authority, in my said County and State, on this the __28__ day of __Nov__, __1997__ .

My commission expires __Feb 8, 2003__ .

Jayne P. Childers
NOTARY PUBLIC

Document 7-Page 5

115

IN THE CIRCUIT COURT OF _____ COUNTY, WEST VIRGINIA

For Clerk's Use Only

IN RE: INVOLUNTARY HOSPITALIZATION OF

Susie E. George

RESPONDENT

CASE NUMBER: _____ · MH ·

CERTIFICATE OF LICENSED PHYSICIAN/PSYCHOLOGIST

West Virginia Code §§ 27-5-2, 3 & 4

Instructions: *All pages of this certificate must be fully completed.*

I, _Beverley McBride, M.S._ , do hereby certify and state as follows:
(Printed Name of Licensed Physician or Licensed Psychologist)

I have personally observed and examined _____
(Name of Respondent)

on this date and my findings are as follows:

Date of Examination: _11/28/97_ Time: _4.30 pm_

Place of the Examination: _Greenbrier County Sheriff's office_

Lewisburg , _Greenbrier_ West Virginia
(City) (County)

PART A - GENERAL FINDINGS

I find there is reason to believe the Respondent _____ IS _✓_ IS NOT

[✓] mentally ill   [✓] mentally retarded   [✓] addicted to alcohol or drugs

The specific symptoms and behavior on which this finding is based are:

Domestic strife between Mrs. George and
daughter re: care of Mrs. George Retarded
dau. Mrs. George just diag. of cancer

SCA-511903-1 / 4-97

Document 7-Page 6

116

I further find that the Respondent _____ IS __✓__ IS NOT likely to cause serious harm to him/herself or others as a result of such condition because of the following recent overt behavior:

Pt is in a stressful situation at home
and at odds with dau. and son-in-law
They are also under stress.

Based on such examination, I therefore certify as follows [initial only ONE of the following recommendations]:

_____ The Respondent should be committed for further evaluation pursuant to § 27-5-3 [probable cause hearing only]

_____ The Respondent should be finally committed pursuant to § 27-5-4 (k) for a temporary observation period (TOP) not to exceed six (6) months [final commitment hearing only]

_____ The Respondent should be finally committed for an indeterminate period pursuant to § 27-5-4 (k) [final commitment hearing only]

___✓___ The Respondent does not require hospitalization [probable cause or final commitment hearing]

Information regarding physician or psychologist completing this certificate:

Name: ___BEVERLEY McBRIDE MS.___
                    (please print or type)

Address: ___LEWISBURG___ ___WV___ Telephone Number: ___304 645-3648___
            (city)   (state)   (zip)

                [ ] Medicine
License to practice [ ] Osteopathy   Registration/License Number: ___95___
                [ ] Psychology

Signature: ___Beverly McBride, MS___ Date: ___11/28/97___

Document 7-Page 7

117

5. Subscale Scores of the *[check one]* ____ BPRS or the ____ BPRS-C:

Score	BPRS Subscale
	Somatization/Anxiety/Depression
✓	Hostility/Suspiciousness
	Thinking Disturbance
	Withdrawal/Blunt Affect/Motor Retardation
	Excitement/Tension/Distractibility/ Hyperactivity
	Bizarre Behavior/ Mannerisms/Neglect
	Total Subscale Score

Score	BPRS-C Subscale
	Behavior Problems
	Depression
	Thinking Disturbance
	Psychomotor Agitation
	Withdrawal/ Retardation
	Anxiety
	Organicity
	Total Subscale Score

Sn in last dau: have been on doubling up on antidepr + causing ... may be ... approach

6. The results of my evaluation suggest the following substance abuse symptoms are present *[check all that apply]*:

Symptom(s)	Yes	No	General Information
Periodic, Frequent or Constant Substance Use		—	Type: Amount:
Public Intoxication Charges		✓	Frequency in Past 90 Days:
Substance Abuse to the Point of Incapacitation		✓	Explain:
Employment Instability		✓	Explain:

7. Overall Impressions: _Elderly lady under extreme stress w. dx cancer + care of 51 yr old retarded daughter._

Document 7-Page 8

118

DSM - Diagnostic Impression (include all five axes):

Pt had previous dx of Major Depres

presently under tx with Zoloft &

Xanax. Does not show symptoms at

this time. Family needs therapy/

medication.

Clinician Rating of Treatment Needs [circle your impression]:

0	1	2	3	4
No observable seriously suicidal behavior (SHB)	Slight probability of SHB.	Mild probability of SHB. Crisis residential unit (CRU) appropriate	Moderate probability of SHB	High probability SHB. Should be monitored until hospitalized
No treatment needed.	Outpatient therapies needed.	24-hour supervision needed.	Immediate hospitalization in a 24-hour locked facility needed.	Immediate hospitalization a 24-hour locked facility needed.

Physician/Psychologist Signature: _____ Date: 4/28/97

Document 7-Page 9

119

IN THE CIRCUIT COURT OF _Greenbrier_ COUNTY, WEST VIRGINIA

IN RE: Involuntary Hospitalization of   Case No. : _97-MH-48_

Susie E. Greene George
                    RESPONDENT

ORDER:
NO PROBABLE CAUSE FOR INVOLUNTARY HOSPITALIZATION FOR EXAMINATION
[W.Va. Code §27-5-2(b)(5)]

This matter was heard on the _28th_ day of _November, 1997_ . The Applicant,

Janice Rebecca Jones , appeared in person and was represented by

_____ , Assistant/Prosecuting Attorney of _____

County, West Virginia.   The respondent appeared in person and was represented by counsel,
Eric M. Frantis .

After hearing the testimony of witnesses and receiving all relevant evidence, examining the written report and certification

/ said psychologist / physician, and hearing the arguments of counsel, the Court FINDS (initial appropriate items):

The Respondent ___ IS ___ IS NOT a resident of this County.

The Respondent ___ WAS ___ WAS NOT found in this County.

There is [initial appropriate item(s)]:

___ PROBABLE CAUSE ___ NO PROBABLE CAUSE to believe the Respondent is addicted;

___ PROBABLE CAUSE ___ NO PROBABLE CAUSE to believe the Respondent is mentally ill;

___ PROBABLE CAUSE ___ NO PROBABLE CAUSE to believe the Respondent is mentally retarded.

This Court also FINDS probable cause to believe the Respondent (initial one) ___ IS ___ IS NOT likely to cause

serious harm to self and/or others because of such mental illness or mental retardation if allowed to remain at liberty.

MHB _07_ PAGE _65_

Document 7-Page 10

120

REVOCATION OF POWER OF ATTORNEY

Know all men by these presences, that, whereas, in and by my Power of Attorney, I, SUSIE GEORGE, did make, constitute and appoint Rebecca Jones and/or David George, my true and lawful attorneys for me, and in my name, place and stead to act in my name and place and for my benefit on my behalf, as more fully appear by reference to said Power of Attorney.

Now, therefore, I, the said SUSIE GEORGE, do hereby revoke, countermand, annul and make void the said Power of Attorney in the above mentioned and all power of authority thereby given or intended to be given to the said Rebecca Jones and/or David George, Power of Attorney of record in the Office of the County Clerk of the County Commission of Greenbrier County, West Virginia, in Power of Attorney Book 14 at page 619..

IT WITNESS THEREOF, I have hereunto set my hand this the 9th day of December, 1997.

Susie George
SUSIE GEORGE

STATE OF WEST VIRGINIA,

COUNTY OF GREENBRIER, to-wit:

I, Lora Mitchell, the undersigned Notary Public acknowledge that SUSIE GEORGE, signed the foregoing Revocation of Power of Attorney before me and in my presence this the 9th day of December, 1997.

My commission expires: 12-5-00

(Seal)
OFFICIAL SEAL
NOTARY PUBLIC
STATE OF WEST VIRGINIA
LORA MITCHELL
BOX 184 HARTS SOCK RD.
CLINTONVILLE, WV 24928
My Commission Expires December 5, 2000

Lora Mitchell
Notary Public

Document 8-Page 1

121

and make void the said Power of Attorney in the above mentioned and all power of authority thereby given or intended to be given to the said Rebecca Jones and/or David George, Power of Attorney of record in the Office of the County Clerk of the County Commission of Greenbrier County, West Virginia, in Power of Attorney Book 14 at page 619.

IT WITNESS THEREOF, I have hereunto set my hand this the 9th day of December, 1997.

_____
SUSIE GEORGE

STATE OF WEST VIRGINIA,

COUNTY OF GREENBRIER, to-wit:

I, _Lora Mitchell_____, the undersigned Notary Public acknowledge that SUSIE GEORGE, signed the foregoing Revocation of Power of Attorney before me and in my presence this the 9th day of December, 1997.

My commission expires: 12-5-00

_____
Notary Public

BARRY L. BRUCE
AND ASSOCIATES
ATTORNEYS AT LAW
P.O. BOX 388
LEWISBURG, WV 24901

This instrument was prepared by the law firm of Barry L. Bruce & Associates, P.O. Box 388, 101 W. Randolph St., Lewisburg, West Virginia.

Document 8-Page 2

122

Fee $3.00 Return to: Barry Bruce

VOLUNTARY REVOCATION OF POWER OF ATTORNEY

KNOW ALL MEN BY THESE PRESENCE, that in and by that certain Power of Attorney dated February 7, 1997, executed by Patty George, the undersigned, REBECCA JONES, was named as true and lawful attorney for Patty George.

Now, therefore, I, REBECCA JONES, hereby voluntarily resign as Power of Attorney for Patty George and revoke, countermand, annul and make void the said Power of Attorney and all power of authority thereby given or intended to be given to the said REBECCA JONES under the Power of Attorney placed of record in the Office of the Clerk of the County Commission of Greenbrier County, West Virginia in Power of Attorney Book 14 at page 764.

IN WITNESS WHEREOF, I have hereunto set my hand this the 15 day of ~~December~~ January, 199~~7~~8.

Rebecca Jones
REBECCA JONES

STATE OF WEST VIRGINIA,

COUNTY OF GREENBRIER, TO WIT:

I, Jerry Manchin, the undersigned Notary Public acknowledge that REBECCA JONES, signed the foregoing Voluntary Revocation of Power of Attorney before me and in my presence this the 15 day of ~~December 1997.~~ January 1998.

My commission expires: 10-11-1999

OFFICIAL SEAL
NOTARY PUBLIC
STATE OF WEST VIRGINIA
JERRY MANCHIN
P C Box 1926
Huntington WV

Notary Public

Prepared by: ~~Barry L. Bruce~~ and Associates, PO Box 388,

Document 9- Page 1

123

lawful attorney for Patty George.

Now, therefore, I, REBECCA JONES, hereby voluntarily resign as Power of Attorney for Patty George and revoke, countermand, annul and make void the said Power of Attorney and all power of authority thereby given or intended to be given to the said REBECCA JONES under the Power of Attorney placed of record in the Office of the Clerk of the County Commission of Greenbrier County, West Virginia in Power of Attorney Book 14 at page 764.

IN WITNESS WHEREOF, I have hereunto set my hand this the 15 day of ~~December~~, *January*, 199~~7~~8.

Rebecca Jones
REBECCA JONES

STATE OF WEST VIRGINIA,

COUNTY OF GREENBRIER, TO WIT:

I, _Jerry Manchin_, the undersigned Notary Public acknowledge that REBECCA JONES, signed the foregoing Voluntary Revocation of Power of Attorney before me and in my presence this the 15 day of ~~December 1997~~ *January 1998*.

My commission expires: _10-11-1999_

Notary Public

OFFICIAL SEAL
NOTARY PUBLIC
STATE OF WEST VIRGINIA
JERRY MANCHAM
P. O. Box 1995
Huntington, WV
My Commission Expires 11

Prepared By: ~~Barry L. Bruce~~ and Associates, PO Box 388,

Lewisburg WV 24901

WEST VIRGINIA, Greenbrier County, S. S:
In the Clerk's Office of Greenbrier County Court _16th_ day of _Jan._ 199_8_
This _____ was this day presented in the office aforesaid and thereupon, together with the Certificate thereto annexed, admitted to record.
Teste _Sandra Magan_ Clerk
By _Rebecca S. Sigmorez_ Deputy

BOOK 15 PAGE 251

Document 9-Page 2

124

Last Will and Testament

OF

SUSIE E. GEORGE

I, SUSIE E. GEORGE, a resident of and domiciled at P. O. Box 93, Quinwood, Greenbrier

County, West Virginia do hereby make, publish and declare this to be my Last Will and Testament,

hereby revoking all previous wills and testamentary dispositions made by me.

ARTICLE I. I am a widow and I have six (6) children; namely, Connie Bennett, Nancy

Richmond, David George, Janice Rebecca Jones, Mary Holloway and Patty Sue George.

ARTICLE II. I direct that all my just debts and funeral expenses be paid or provided for as

soon as practicable after my death.

ARTICLE III. All estate and inheritance taxes or transfer or death taxes which may be

assessed or imposed with respect to my estate or any part thereof, wheresoever situated, whether or

not passing under this will, including the taxable value of all policies of insurance on my life and all

transfers, powers, rights or interests includable in my estate for the purpose of such taxes, shall be

paid out of my residuary estate as an expense of administration and without apportionment and shall

not be prorated or charged against any of the other gifts in this Will or against property not passing

under this Will.

Document 10-Page 1

125

ARTICLE IV. I direct that any gift or transfer which I have made or may hereafter make during my lifetime to any beneficiary under this Will shall not be treated as an advancement.

ARTICLE V. I give, devise and bequeath unto my legally incapacitated and incompetent daughter, Patty Sue George, all the rest, residue and remainder of my estate, real, personal, and mixed, wheresoever situate and of whatsoever kind. I direct that my daughters, Connie Bennett and Nancy Richmond be appointed as Co-Guardians of her person and that the Trust Department of First State Bank, Rainelle, West Virginia be Trustee of her estate. The Trustee of the Estate of my daughter, Patty Sue George, is authorized at its discretion and without authorization by any Court:

A) To defer payment or distribution of the whole or any part of such property and to hold and invest same for such incompetent daughter;

B) To pay, distribute or apply any part of such property or any income therefrom for the care, comfort, maintenance, support, use or other benefit of said incompetent, either directly or by making distribution thereof to the personal guardian, committee or other legal representative of such incompetent or to such person with whom she shall reside. Should

Document 10-Page 2

Patty Sue George die before distribution of all the property held under this article, then I direct that the Trustee and Executor shall make distribution of the remainder to my surviving devisees as stated hereafter; and

C) To permit the incompetent and the Guardian of her person to have the use and possession of any real or tangible personal property necessary to the well being of Patty Sue George.

ARTICLE VI. Should my daughter, Patty Sue George, predecease me, then I give, devise and bequeath unto my surviving children, per capita, all the rest, residue and remainder of my estate, real, personal and mixed, wheresoever situate and of whatsoever kind, to be divided equally among them.

ARTICLE VII. I appoint Connie Bennett and Nancy Richmond, as Co-Executors of this my Last Will and Testament.

ARTICLE VIII. I direct that no security or bond shall be required of any Executor acting hereunder.

IN WITNESS WHEREOF, I have hereunto set my hand and seal to this my Last Will and Testament, which is written without any interlineations on two (2) sheets of paper, to each of which I have subscribed my name. All done in the City of Lewisburg, Greenbrier County, West Virginia, this the 9th day of December, 1997.

Susie E. George (Seal)
SUSIE E. GEORGE

Document 10-Page 3

127

WITNESSES:-

[signatures]

STATE OF WEST VIRGINIA

COUNTY OF GREENBRIER, TO-WIT:

This day personally appeared before me, the undersigned, the three witnesses whose names are signed below, who after being by me first duly sworn, did say that the foregoing instrument contained on two (2) sheets of paper was on the _9th_ day of _December_, 1997, signed and sealed SUSIE E. GEORGE, the Testatrix herein named and duly published and declared

Document 10-Page 4

by her to be her Last Will and Testament and her free act and deed in the presence of them who at her request and in her presence and in the presence of each other did subscribe their names as witnesses, and they and each of them also did certify and state that the signature of said Testatrix was duly made and appeared to them on the Will before they signed as witnesses as aforesaid, and that they and each of them do believe said Testatrix to be at this time of sound mind and memory.

Subscribed and sworn to before me a Notary Public in and for the County and State aforesaid this the 9th day of December, 1997.

My commission expires: 12-5-00

(Seal)

_____
Notary Public

This instrument prepared by the law firm of Barry L. Bruce & Associates, P.O. Box 388, Lewisburg, WV 24901.

Document 10-Page 5

129

FILE NO;12870

WEST VIRGINIA, Greenbrier County Commission Clerk's Office
April 16,1998.

A paper writing purporting to be the Last Will and
Testament of Susie E. George , deceased, was this
day presented before R. Sandra Morgan, Clerk of the County
Commission, in her office and was proven by affidavit taken
before Lora Mitchell , a Notary Public, in and for
Greenbrier County, of Jerry Markham, Tamara Wagner and
Whitney L. Meriwether , witnesses to said Will, it is
hereby ORDERED that the said paper be recorded as the Last
Will and Testament of Susie E. George , deceased.

TESTE: R. Sandra Morgan CLERK.

Document 10-Page 6

130

Fee $3.50 Mail to: Nancy Richmond
Box 152
Quinwood, WV 25981

MAR 2 ~

DURABLE POWER OF ATTORNEY

I, SUSIE E. GEORGE, residing at Quinwood, Greenbrier County, West Virginia, hereby

appoint CONNIE BENNETT and NANCY RICHMOND, Greenbrier County, West Virginia, as my

Attorneys-in-Fact, to act in my name and place, and for my benefit on my behalf, with authority to

do the following:

1.   Open, maintain or close bank accounts (including, but not limited to checking

accounts, savings accounts and certificates of deposit), brokerage accounts, and other similar

accounts with financial institutions.

a. Conduct any business with any banking or financial institution with respect to any
of my accounts, including but not limited to, making deposits and withdrawals,
obtaining bank statements, passbooks, drafts, money orders, warrants and certificates
or vouchers payable to me by any person, firm, corporation or political entity.

b. Perform any act necessary to deposit, negotiate, sell, or transfer any note, security,
or draft of the United States of America, including U.S. Treasury Securities.

c. Have access to any safety deposit box that I might own, including its contents.

2.   Sell, exchange, buy, invest, or reinvest any assets or property owned by me.

Document 11-Page 1

131

3.   Take any and all legal steps necessary to collect any claim amount or debt owed to me, or to settle any claim, whether made against me or asserted on my behalf against any other person or entity.

4.   Enter into binding contracts on my behalf.

5.   Sell, convey, lease, mortgage, manage, insure, improve, repair, or perform any other act with respect to any of my property (now owned or later acquired), including but not limited to, real estate and real estate rights (including the right to remove tenants and to recover possession).

6.   Prepare, sign, and file documents with any governmental body or agency, including but not limited to, authorization to:

a. Prepare, sign and file income and other tax returns with federal, state and local and other governmental bodies.

b. Obtain information or documents from any government or its agencies, and negotiate, compromise, or settle any matter with such government or agency.

c. Prepare applications, provide information, and perform any other act reasonably requested by any government or its agencies in connection with governmental benefits.

7.   I also authorize my representative to act on my behalf to give, withhold or withdraw

Document 11-Page 2

132

informed consent to health care decisions in the event that I an not able to do so myself.

This appointment shall extend to (but not be limited to) decisions relating to medical treatment, surgical treatment, nursing care, medication, hospitalization, care and treatment in a nursing home or other facility, and home health care. The representative appointed by this document is specifically authorized to act on my behalf to consent to. refuse or withdraw any and all medical treatment or diagnostic procedures, if my representative determines that I, if able to do so, would consent to, refuse or withdraw such treatment or procedures. Such authority shall not be limited to, the withholding or withdrawal of life-prolonging intervention when in the opinion of two physicians who have examined me, one of whom is my attending physician, such life-prolonging intervention offers no medical hope of benefit.

This Power of Attorney shall become effective upon the disability or incapacity of the principal.

I hereby grant to my Attorneys-in-Fact full right, power and authority to do ever act, deed and thing necessary or advisable to be done concerning the above powers, as fully as I could do if

Document 11-Page 3

133

personally present and acting.

This Power of Attorney shall become effective immediately, shall not be affected by any disability or lack of mental competence, and shall continue effective until my death; provided, however, that this Power may be revoked by me as to my Attorneys-in-Fact at any time by written notice to my Attorneys-in-Fact.

Dated this the 9th day of December, 1997, at Lewisburg, Greenbrier County, West Virginia.

Susie E. George
SUSIE E. GEORGE

I did not sign the principal's signature above. I an at least eighteen years of age and am not related to the principal by blood or marriage. I am not entitled to any portion of the estate of the principal according to the laws of intestate succession of the state of the principal's domicile or to the best of my knowledge under any will of the principal or codicil thereto, or legally responsible for the costs of the principal's medical or other care. I am not the principal's attending physician, nor am I the representative or successor representative of the principal.

Document 11-Page 4

DATE:

Tamara Wagner   12-9-97

Whitney L. Merewether   12-9-97

STATE OF WEST VIRGINIA

COUNTY OF GREENBRIER, TO-WIT:

I, _Lora Mitchell_ , a Notary Public of said County and State, do certify

SUSIE E. GEORGE, as principal, and _Tamara Wagner_ and

Whitney L. Merewether as witnesses, whose names are signed to the writing above have this

day acknowledged the same before me.

Given under my hand this _9th_ day of _December_, 1997.

My commission expires: _12-5-00_

OFFICIAL SEAL
NOTARY PUBLIC
STATE OF WEST VIRGINIA
LORA MITCHELL
BOX 184 HEARTBREAK RD.
CLINTONVILLE, WV 24928
My Commission Expires December 5, 2000

Lora Mitchell
Notary Public

Document 11-Page 5

135

This instrument prepared by the law firm of Barry L. Bruce and Associates, P. O. Box 388, Lewisburg, WV 24901.

WEST VIRGINIA, Greenbrier County, S. S:
In the Clerk's Office of Greenbrier County Court ____17th____ day of __March__ 1998
This ____Plat____ was this day presented in the office aforesaid and thereupon, together with the Certificate thereto annexed, admitted to record.

Teste __R. Sandra Mogen__ Clerk

By __Delenn S. Lightner__ Deputy

BOOK **15** PAGE **279**

Document 11-Page 6

136

BARRY L. BRUCE AND ASSOCIATES

P.O. BOX 388
101 W. RANDOLPH STREET
LEWISBURG, WEST VIRGINIA 24901
TELEPHONE: (304) 645-4182 • TELECOPIER: (304) 645-4183

BARRY L. BRUCE
also, member of Ohio Bar
E. LAVOYD MORGAN, JR.
Attorneys at Law

December 16, 1997

JERRY MARKHAM
BECKY GODBY
Legal Assistants

Ms. Rebecca Jones
P. O. Box 44   and
Quinwood WV 25981

Mr. David George
22189 Westview Avenue
Brooke Park OH 44142

SUBJECT: SUSIE GEORGE AND PATTY GEORGE

Dear Ms. Jones and Mr. George:

This law firm represents the above subject in regard to various matters, including the properties of her estate and revocations of certain powers of attorney.

Enclosed for your information and records is a Revocation of Power of Attorney wherein Ms. George has elected to revoke that certain power of attorney naming you as her joint attorneys in fact. This document has been placed of record in the Office of the Clerk of the County Commission in Book 15 at page 224, and the power of attorney given to you is now null and void.

We have also obtained a copy of the Power of Attorney given to you by Patty George on or about February 7, 1997. Enclosed is a Voluntary Revocation of that Power of Attorney which we would appreciate your signing before a Notary Public and returning to us promptly for recording. As you are aware, Patty is an incapacitated, incompetent person and is unable to legally execute a Power of Attorney. It is not our desire to file a legal action to have the Power of Attorney revoked; however, we will have no alternative if you elect not to sign the enclosed Voluntary Revocation.

Document 12-Page 1

137

We are also enclosing a Deed for your signature before a Notary Public. By signing this Deed, you are conveying all your right, title and interest in and to Ms. George's property to her, where it rightfully belongs. Likewise, it is not our desire to file any legal action to obtain possession of the property on behalf of Ms. George; however, if the deed is not executed by you, then we will have no other alternative.

We look forward to your prompt cooperation and return of these signed, notarized documents. Thank you.

Yours very truly,

Barry L. Bruce
Attorney at Law

Enclosures

cc: Susie George

Document 12-Page 2

Greenbrier Valley Nat'l Bank
Lewisburg, WV

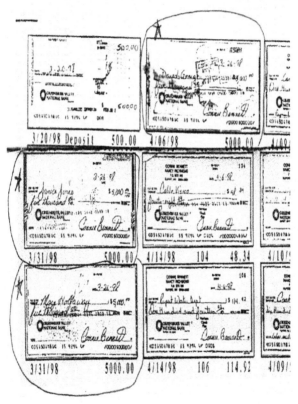

Document 13

139

IN THE CIRCUIT COURT OF GREENBRIER COUNTY, WEST VIRGINIA

IN RE: PATSY SUE GEORGE   CASE NO. 98-G-16
    A Protected Person

ORDER

This matter came on for hearing before the Court on November 4, 1999, upon the Petition

for Removal of Connie Bennett as Guardian and for Appointment of Conservator and Successor

Guardian, previously filed herein by Rebecca Jones. Present were Rebecca Jones, Mary Holloway

and David George, in person and by their attorney, Robert E. Richardson; Connie Bennett, in person

and by her attorney, Jeffrey S. Rodgers; and Patsy Sue George, by Eric H. Francis, her guardian ad

litem. Nancy Richmond was also present for portions of the hearing, in person but without counsel..

Upon consideration of the said Petition, the Orders previously entered herein, the evidence

presented, the argument of counsel, and all other information of record in this proceeding, the Court

does find that Connie Bennett has previously been appointed as guardian of Patsy Sue George,

Document 14-Page 1

the said Connie Bennett has failed and refused to comply with the Court's Orders entered herein on

May 4, 1999, and on July 29, 1999, following hearings conducted on December 30, 1998, and July

19, 1999, respectively; and that it is in the best interest of the said Patsy Sue George that Connie

Bennett be removed as her guardian and that Rebecca Jones be appointed in her place and stead as

such guardian. Accordingly, it is ADJUDGED, ORDERED and DECREED that Connie Bennett

is hereby REMOVED as guardian for Patsy Sue George, a protected person, and that Rebecca Jones

is appointed in her place and stead as such guardian.

Document 14-Page 2

About The Author

Nancy Richmond is an award winning author who has been writing professionally for over thirty years, as a newspaper and magazine columnist and as the author of fifteen books. A historian and a certified genealogist, Nancy is a member of the Greenbrier Historical Society and the West Virginia Writers, Inc. Her books can be found at Tamarack in Beckley, WV and at the Open Book bookstore and the North House Museum in Lewisburg, WV, as well as at Amazon.com and numerous other book store sites on the internet. For more information on the author and her books, please visit

nancyrichmondbooks.com

CPSIA information can be obtained
at www.ICGtesting.com
Printed in the USA
BVOW06s1920101116
467518BV00010B/207/P